GREYHOUND AMERICANS

MONCHO OLLIN ALVARADO

saturnalia | BOOKS

Distributed by Independent Publishers Group
Chicago

Saturnalia Books
105 Woodside Rd.
Ardmore, PA 19003
info@saturnaliabooks.com

ISBN: 978-1-947817-36-4 (print), 978-1-947817-37-1 (ebook)
Library of Congress Control Number: 2021947112

Book design by Robin Vuchnich
Cover Art by Oscar Ochoa

Distributed by:
Independent Publishing Group
814 N. Franklin St.
Chicago, IL 60610
800-888-4741

Para mi familia, mi antepasadxs, y para ti
Without you, there wouldn't be flower songs

CONTENTS

III

IV

V

Los Caminos de la vida
No son como yo pensaba
Como los imaginaba
No son como yo creía

—Omar Antonio Geles Suarez

I am memory alive

—Joy Harjo

Self-Portrait with *La Sonora Dinamita* Playing in the Background

a flower in the hair   magic

the words   a spell where gods live

my throat   my first instrument

a harvest of invisible truths

of particles   quarks   light waves

I dance the way a cactus chokes the sun

my breath   a butterfly in sky

that will know everyone again & again

mouth   why do you hold so much

this is how it happens   *tonacayo*

flesh   possessed by suddens

how watermelon seeds are surrounded by earth

they contain so much whole   they rise

from the ground   bulbous   *vida   viva*

universe   speak my name

break me open

with all that sound

I

Sift

In elementary dad gave me *Don Pedro* & Coke
gave it to me slowly   like sipping from Christ's cup
He left me with Manny   in a green bedroom

at the Hotel 8   on San Fernando Rd
t.v. buzzing   white noise
door   clicks

Manny's hands   toilet paper soft
strong   enough to touch
weak   enough to rip

It'll be   fine
he   whispered
hold on
            pull

forwards
backwards
don't let go
            don't
                    don't

A night in a friend's pool   during high school
light outside looked   like Manny's room
no moon

just light years
I jumped   breathed in water
saw stars

oscillate
After Manny
dad took me out for *tortas*

said   don't tell *Mari*
I'll buy you   those X-Men toys
Just   don't tell her

At a graveyard guard gig   in college
I shined light   on a galaxy of grass
Then I saw a deer look at me
                    I at him

eyes   became my dad's eyes
when he handed me   a *torta*
                    &   another X-Men toy

Building the Backyard House with *Abuelo*

after Rafa Esparza's Staring at the Sun

The mix in his hands, our skin
covered with clay, horse dung,
hay, & water, his hands

blend it all together, beauty,
how he makes the light
be buried, be alive, deep

his breaths, "*chito,*" he says, "help,"
my hands, to get it right like him,
start to blend the materials, my knees

bend, my arms & hands shovel
mixture into the square wooden frames,
I move until I can see my shadow

inside the mix, my body
sundried like *abuelo's,* southwest
the wind blows, "come back tomorrow,"

he says, & again, I'm there in the bricks,
his voice calls out to me, "a home
in the end, walls, for now,

so it can hold it up," my hands
hold a piece of yesterday, they stick
embracing one another, he coughs

into the bones of his body, his hands,
memories always setting, *abuelo,*
where did you begin & I end

At Eight

Pops, love from you was fists
against my ribs, you called it discipline,

initiation, like your father did to you.
Outside our home was a ten-foot fence

for me to punch, kick, shake, scream
but I leaned my face into rows of rust,

its mesh held me, & I began to sing
the only song I knew, *de colores,*

de colores es el arco iris que vemos lucir.
In my room I looked at myself in the mirror,

the word comes from the Latin, *Mirari,* to wonder,
to miracle from self, my first lesson:

look at everything, how it guides me
to remember, how the body keeps the score,

like earth's crust keeps the records of history:
the bones of all that lived, weapons

we used on ourselves, the plastic that'll take years
& years to decompose, your gold tooth,

your Levi's 501 jeans, your muscle t-shirts,
your hands finally open, quiet

from all the noise they caused

My *Amá* After, a Portrait

Pues at 4:30 am I wait for the bus

to dust mahogany tables scrub granite kitchen tops

sweep & mop marble floors   throw away hair & dead skin

wash & shine windows   dust & vacuum curtains

homeowners never home   except me

& José José singing   *tengo   tanto sentimientos*

Pues   I have dreams of earth opening

the dead rising   inside of homes

office buildings   farm fields

trying to speak

I awaken

with my ginger root hands

empty

& full of ache

Abecedarian Payday Inside the Projects

Alberto's taco stand caramelizes animals on grills, their bodies spirited
away in steam || B train's whistle & piston cuts the city in half || *Carlos*
the *churro* guy cranks dough: it crackles as it meets oil || *Diego*

holds a roll of million-dollar scratchers, sucks his teeth as he quarters
every card || *Efrin,* with a Lakers hoodie, rattles a cart full of cans
up *Pala* St. || *Francisco,* the six-pack philosopher, watches dandelions

heads hit pavement || *Gabriel's familia* leaves a lit *Virgen* candle
under the freeway on Lehigh || Hoyt St. mural has butterflies break
through borders || *Isaac's tía* sells *micheladas* from her '95 Honda trunk

|| Junior's family visits home at *El Michoacano,* eat *tortas de carnitas*
with both hands || *Karla* strums her guitar, the chords vibrate the eyes
inside of me || *Leo* limps street to street to street to street to street

|| Mr. Rogers on PBS teaches my cousin about colors & jazz || Norris St.
makes you feel like an ant at the edge of Earth || *Octavio* shows friends
nightstick bruises, saying, "I vomited beans & rice" || Police scan streets

like birds look for seeds || *Quetzalcoatl* fades on *Tío Chuy's* chest || *Raúl* says, "pops, rehabs about refresh your yesterdays with todays" || Self-portrait of *Frida Kahlo* watches over our little garden of roses ||

Tía & amá sing Paquita, "me estás oyendo inútil, cuánto te odio y te desprecio" || "*Uri,* UFO!" "No foo, it's the ISS, it's going imperceptible" || Van Nuys bus stop has a *veterano* with legs like *chorizo,* who waits

in his wheelchair || *Willie* washes cars on Pala St. & sings, "*dame la fuerza para vivir, un día a la vez*" || *Xitllali's* thumbs pierce an orange, the citrus sprays like a geyser || *Yolli* yells, "do we live in a zoo?"

September 1996

I hear stucco ceiling   scream
like an accordion stretching a note

pops holds her   on the floor
her hands trying to fly

but they limp   become brushes
soaking up carpet

swollen   in red
he throws her outside

all I see is   a blur
the way a comet screeches

he slams doors   shut
his eyes solo cups collecting rain

he says if you let her   in
you'll be turned off like a flashlight

in bed with eyes   closed
I dream of a *piñata's* candies

cascading from its chest   I wake
& slide the door open

amá
my right ear to your back

with both of my arms   drag
her inside the living room

click on the t.v.   hold her
like fire does to wood

Helping my *Amá* Practice for her Citizenship Test

Name: Maricela Alvarado

1.   What does the constitution do?

      Sets, protects, defines rights,
      like how oceans contain
      all that life within

2.   Ideas of sovereignty are in the first three words of the Constitution.
      What are these?

      The we people

3.   How many amendments does the constitution have?

      Twenty-seven, & at twenty-seven weeks of pregnancy,
      you my *chito*, in my belly weighed two pounds,
      as much as a brown baby eagle

4.   What are two rights in the Declaration of Independence?

      Somos Indios de México, we were born with declaration & independence

5.   What is freedom of religion?

      These trees, these flowers, the grass, look how free of religion they are

6.   What is the "rule of law"?

     Your *abuelo* says paper & ink
     owns this piece of land,
     a body owned that grows
     navel oranges
     we eat & drink

7.   Name problems that led to the Civil War

     Pues, slavery

8.   Who lived in New York City before the Europeans arrived?

     Lenape, Hìtkuk, Muhheakantuck, Ahtu

9.   What promises would you make when you become a
     United States citizen?

     Pray, love, vote, protest

10. Name one state that borders *México*

     Tu, my child

Pigeons

they dive & I can't look away, like I couldn't stop looking

your heart rates *abuelo.*

When I last saw you, it was only us & you said, "All my friends

are smiling." *Abuelo*

do they speak *espanól* or English? "They're saying let go of the tongue,

the heart,

don't cry or you'll soon water the valley." *Ay pues,* I tried

abuelo

remember you taught me about *Temicxoch,* dream songs of flowers

sing

& drink light of days in silence, as most of what has lost has lived.

Abuelo

the Earth revolves counterclockwise around the sun, yet, the clocks on earth

move

clockwise, & our ancestors said the present was a reflection of the past.

Abuelo

scientists say the universe will live $T = 10$ raised to the 92nd power minus

infinity years.

Stars die, protons decay, & there will be a period, like at the end of a sentence.

Abuelo,

the next day, a little me saw your empty bed, a window to the

outside,

a steady sound of coos, & I was lost in the edges of the sun.

Abuelo

Hot Cheetos *con Queso*

Mi amor de mi vida, nature,
who knew you tasted this good,

the type of good when they're in me,
my mouth swallows all that life,

this relationship can work out after all,
he & she & they & ze don't care I have

border line personality disorder, but they do,
they leave, & I always come back to you

mi pariente, mi chingon de chingones,
I'm crying into you again,

I was hoping the last time was last,
my therapist said it's because of me

not dealing with my PTSD, trauma, abandonment
issues, I say, naaaaaaaaaaaaaaaaaaaaaaaaaaaa

aaaaaaaaaaw, but I must be honest, loving
people is the most dangerous thing

next to loving myself, a house of spirits
lives within me, all of us, from bacteria

to fish to reptiles to great apes soaring
in space, we don't even know where

we came from, how we got here,
what made all of this, & you:

crunchy corn puffs, red hot powder, hot
jalapeño queso, & *Chavela Vargas* starts singing,

ojala que te vaya bonito. The bag, it's empty,
except, there's a bit of *queso*— beloved,

mi amor de amores,
I think I'm in love
                    with everything

Amá Teaches Me How to Whistle

She said, it's *facil*, look up, kiss everything,
hold the sun between your mouth,

blow like this * *   * *   * ****
****   * *   * * ****   ****

after I told her I was a woman, she wrinkled
the space between us by hugging me.

She told me, "you confused?"
I said, is the fire confused when it eats?

& told her, I'm going by she & my real name,
the one I was born with, not given, she said,

"you are not what it says on your driver's license,"
amá, gracias for believing in this ordinary phenomenon,

like the DNA that made grapes, it made them
a million times before, a million times after,

I have one in my mouth, how round this knowledge,
the gush in my mouth: sweet, tart, & bitter, oh *amá*,

I finally learned how to whistle like you:
* *   * *   * ****   ****   * *   * * ****   ****

Three Eagles Flying

after Laura Aguilar's Three Eagles Flying

Eagle 1

Built alive, song of scars, of devoured snakes

a history of camps: ours, & all

men are created equal, even us

detained, like an "&,"enclosed by sky

a wall, a long silent here, here

stars, a familiar beautiful, inside us sings

passports: ink, plastic, paper, deserts, rivers, suns

Eagle 2

is where my English starts

a safe way to be free

in the air

where my Spanish ends

did you leave your name behind

how does a foreign color look like

Eagle 3

our birth certificate: everything around us;

to sing *Selena's como la flor* at every karaoke,

to dance to *rock en español* until our feet & voices are raw

at every nephew's birthday we drink shots of *tequila* with friends & family,

& ancestors: a noun, pronoun; an interstate, a compound word, all of us contains

one hundred trillion cells inside of this body

antepasadxs, when you saw yourselves in a body of water, a reflection looking at you

did you dive inside to search more of you, or did you cry when seeing yourself fly

Dear *Amá,*

This body is an instrument.
You told me to be loud as clouds,

to learn how to be a name that rises,
like steam from *chilaquiles,*

& once the body is all gone,
sing, "*que lindo esta la mañana*

cuando te fuistes." I understand
the word last: a verb, to continue

in time, to remain, the *Don Pedro,*
you remember how it poured

out onto the floor, the smell
of *carnitas,* a song:

"*llego borracho el borracho,*"
is playing the soundtrack to that time,

when pops finally left, 25 years
cried out, I thought I shouldn't

tear so long, it doesn't go away,
it's those spaces on the walls

that've been plastered & painted ripe *mango*,
your eyes looking outside that day:

two butterflies eating
a half-cut orange. Your hands

are smaller than mine, darker
at the ridges of the knuckles,

I hold them between mine,
it opens an ending

Hey Pops,

Since you left, I've lived brown,
down, & queer, in wonder

of how sand speaks of memory,
& is the mother of all wisdom,

what does that make you? I'm becoming
the person of my young dreams,

& you know *Pacoima* means the entrance,
not running water? Have you learned

hands can be used for hugging?
I still can't say *Parangaricutirimicuaro*,

& I still can't stop your collection letters from coming,
they're like horizons: never-ending, always

beginning, like home,
another wound I can't go back to

Happy Father's Day *Amá*

I held forty years of woman in my hands,
feet blazed copper from ten-hour shifts,

massaged VapoRub on your feet, their cracks
scrapes, cuts, corns, blisters, sneaker indents.

The mint would free your breathing:
a bouquet of air,

a bloom I learned
from your every breath:

a simple forever. Your hands
open to all possibilities

when you put anything into them,
like how you would make dinner:

pieces of pork with bone in a broth
of *chile verde* sauce: a savory in shades

the bone velvet,
my tongue opens

the marrow: coarse
& soft like soil,

your sacrifice for me:
a towards, a refusal,

a never, a courage
born with all this, oh *amá*,

I'm still learning light
exhausts into everything,

expecting nothing back,
& I sucked the dying

& let go of words

Is My Life Really Worth 12 Dollars an Hour?

On break I browse wealthy subreddits: gold toilets,

personal jets; the French Revolution started with less,

& it's not that I'm mad, but trees drink water so freely;

& I've tried to write a line after atrocities around the world

but listen to *Juan Gabriel* instead; & about making *tamales,*

my *tía* would say, "Give your name to the *masa,* smooth

the sun rays into the edges," then when *amá* saw me in a dress

she said, "Where's my *chito*?" They're there, among the atoms,

electrons, protons, neutrons; It feels like everybody

pays someone: water to flowers, sun to trees, my checking account

to my college loans; welcome to Tj's, how was your day?

They say, "Good," look at their phones, *pues,* at least at McDees

people talk to screens. We ride tomorrow in a rush of today,

it takes shape in the cosmic invisible going through us,

in, until, away, a together never to return,

but does change do nothing? I've given plenty to customers,

but later I punch-out from work, I remember Ruddy Roye saying, "Life,

is a constant protest— *pues,* I still can't fathom how we'll become ancestors

in the future, how all the roots & seeds of humanity come from a common ancestor, they made me here, made me love, without the weight of ideology,

& our DNA is an opus that unwinds in heroes, rebels, villains, ruins, fossils,

99¢ pinto bean cans, & Carl Sagan saying "Earth, that dot…here…that's home…

that's us…every human being who ever was…" You want paper or plastic?

How I Eat the Stars

I understand how some things live
more than others. I kept throwing up
pills, whiskey, bacon, & the sun,
but a body can surprise us
when it senses something wrong,
it starts to groan,
it knows
I've tried with a blade, different pills
& bourbon, but this time there's no one around,
only trees, sky, flies—gorgeous
how my body keeps me up all night, splendor
the stars, they give themselves
unconditionally,
I lie open, let everything in: a billion years
of consequences, they hold me together,
these old giant trees above me: naked
without any human intervention, until my palms
can't help it but peel the bark, how soft
their skin like they're asleep about to wake,
I eat a piece of them,
I start to root
into the earth, again

A List for Every Time My Depression Tries to Obituary Me

For J

At the end, in the dark, there's a place where words can't be carried.

Look at your hands: brown infinities that can't draw a perfect circle.

It's ok not to remember; whales don't remember all their songs that vibrate seas.

I'm still learning to live the things I didn't have before: self-care & empathy.

An unbearable horizon: the last page turning in your favorite book.

One day I awoke & tried to recall everything.

I'm going to live all my dreams, even the one where I speak sunflower.

It's ok to cry out the borders in you, how many people have cried out today?

Everything's a lesson, just listen, see, smell, taste, & touch, & you'll know.

I have used up all my fears.

Spiritually speaking, we are the stars, we nova, flux, lux.

Panic will try to take the intensity of nows.

Fight it.

Dictionary the world, noun the living, verb memories.

Eat a caramel chew, place it in the roof of your mouth: a sweety-goo that lasts.

Create an energy that will live a thousand generations: my beloveds' lips on mine.

History opens & closes like an accordion, but do you see all this life? The Earth

came from gases, molded into a planet. That is part of a solar system, this system

a part of the Milky Way galaxy, this galaxy a part of the super cluster: *Lanaikea*,

meaning: immense heaven, which resides in this universe that made *amá*,

& she made *capirotada*: *bolillos* in *piloncillo* juice, cloves, cinnamon, raisins,

& you

II

Prima Perita, a Portrait

Mi amor took pictures of cartel heads
splayed like loose beads on the streets

did his last breath leave early between 4 & 5 a.m.
found in pits across the borders   maybe his body

was in a laundry bag   inside a black van   all he saw was:

Primo Hector went up to California   after morning light could be seen
in 14 holes through his apartment wall

In *prima Nena*'s bed   just hair

Did the cartel drive you to the desert   make you dig a hole
your body compressed into a cube of flesh & bone

did you look up at all the empty
& roll in

Tío Urbano Visits *Santa Teresa* Cemetery, a Portrait

Your name written on the top left
                                        I don't want to read it

officials told me it was a drunk hit & run
                                        neighbors said it was the officials

I remembered you were lying there
                                        smell of bleach

roses
                                        sweat

your body molded by tires
                                        the papers had your name

that air   those words   the taste
                                        all I can do

all I ever do
                                        is just place my hand

                    there

I brush leaves away with my feet

moving to *Cumbia* *Merengue* *Salsa*

                    veins

leave the living

it reminds me of your feet

a tree next to you

I strip off dead branches

Primo José, a Portrait

your name   burnt sugar
on the walls   your photos
your teeth   outlasts you
like footprints   left on the moon
no wind   will touch
remember   sky
always has gold

Prima Monse on a Park Bench, a Portrait

you're all leaf with no tree
the way you sway on a bench
divine
how humans can look in the face
the way you're bent
it looks like you're praying
for all of us
then you let go
it scatters the prayer
wordless in the aftermath
you look at the unavoidable
your face looks up as you're being taken
by an uncontrollable laughter
god
how it shook me

Tío Danny, a Portrait

my boy once asked   are there richer versions of us
I tried to write him in a birthday card   a richer version

of me was out once   slanging bags   snortin' sniffin'
wonderin'   why dead portraits of presidents

mean so much more than me   I tried
at social services for a new way of life

but the clerk denies me because I have an expired ID
I guess I need a refreshed portrait in this decade

to live in a season of applications
for people to say   we are always accepting online applications

all I could write was   I know why you don't come around
but I still love you   it left me with emotions

I couldn't afford

Tío Willie Working as a Security Guard, a Portrait

I'm standing on an ancient land   for minimum dollars an hour

in a honeycomb museum   I protect a giant balloon dog

a porcelain boy with a pony   & other times I live in mouths

of people in photographs   what were they saying

& did they know they'll be living suspended on white walls

never knowing any other season   but now

Primo Refugio, a Portrait

Rosary beads on my chest kept me company

click

clickclick

click

two people were laughing

why didn't you have our money

I kissed the concrete

warm piss & gravel

you know what we do & who we are

I saw snake boots & a Ford pickup

black ice on the back of my neck

click

clickclick

click

it still doesn't shoot

tires screeched

I screamed

It was all teeth

My People, a Portrait

Our language is sky & barbed wire
a nectar   an ever you always knew
our gift is an alphabet of shadows
lessons of suns   rainbows
veneration of space & time
a portrait that never humans or gods
always born in molds
we are the dreams of now
never to breathe this moment again
remember   we all return to eternal
time is ending & birthing us all the time
ghosts inhabit the food around us
to feel mouths again
look around   we are not alone
ancestors   aesthetics   equations
say words to keep safe
chrysanthemum   sonder   iridescent
amá said while crossing the border
what madness these clouds

Mi Gente, un Retrato

Nuestro lenguaje es el cielo y el alambre de púas

un néctar   que siempre supiste

nuestro regalo es un alfabeto de sombras

lecciones de soles   arcoíris

veneración del espacio y el tiempo

un retrato que nunca humanos o dioses

siempre nacido en moldes

somos los sueños de ahora

nunca respirar este momento otra vez

recuerda   que todos volvemos a lo eterno

el tiempo se acaba y nos da vida al mismo tiempo

fantasmas habitan comida alredor

para sentir bocas otra ves

mira a nuestro alrededor   no estamos solos

ancestrxs   estéticas   ecuaciones

decir palabras para mantenerse a salvo

crisantemo   sonder   iridiscente

dijo amá mientras cruzaba la frontera

que locura estas nubes

Primo Nacho, a Portrait

As a kid I was taken for a ride
a man was bound in chains in the trunk
my *tío* put a *machete* in my right hand
pressed it against the man's throat
my hand trembled
my *tío* pushed in my arm
my eyes closed
all I heard were rattles
the smell afterwards
I remember all day
a child swinging left
to right
the sky
so blue
it blinds

Primo Jesús Works on *Taco* Tuesday, a Portrait

Today is the ten thousandth seven hundredth
& seventh day I've been alive   again guys
in polo shirts with khakis ask for cups of water
just buy a small drink it's only a dollar

even people waiting outside of Home Depot pay
then senior citizens call me *José* or *Juan*
my name is *Jesús* for Christ sake

& in the afternoon Devin comes by   smells
like baby wipes   blue cheese
his hands reek of metal

he asks how it feels preparing foreign food
at night lonely people in their cars eat twelve *tacos*
I pick up brown bags   empty wrappers
everything eaten but the shells   & after

cooking six hundred & fifty-five soft chicken *tacos*
a quote greases in my head   I cannot remember the books I read
like the meals I have eaten   even so   they have made me

The next morning lightning struck our store
everything went plasma   I saw roots
in the sky   stuck between two worlds

Dear *Amá*,

How do you hold the brokenness of your life? I recall you saying you're afraid of people, minds, & death. Trans women without papers disappear in this country by I.C.E. & all they want is to be free, to have a voice, to laugh, to have a name. I had enough *Amá,* so I went to the biggest protests of my life: students from all over California walked, sang, chanted; some carrying red flags, with a black eagle in the middle, then *Mexica* dancers dressed as jaguars sang *"Nantli! Tlen atl moyolo, ilea tlauili, tijtemitia noixtiyol"* A river of humanity washed over the streets into the city center square. Speeches were full of fruit, some bitter, mostly sweet, they overcame the crowd & me. During all of this, I finally understood my *tia's* name: *Esperanza*, hope; the word swallowed me, like how it feels being inside the Ocean.

      I yelled with everyone, give them back! Give them back!"
My scream potent as cardamom, but then I saw drones above us, cops with guns & armor surrounding the buildings—I felt like a word on a page in a U.S. history book. You said on October 2, 1968, in Mexico City, students, workers, & the poor protested, saying "'we don't want Olympics, we want a revolution!" more than six hundred students were massacred, names on a chalk board, erased. Guns & drones & more guns pointing down at them, at us, I started to vanish the faces of the crowds, the children on their parents' shoulders. Then something happened: nothing, the speeches were finished & they told everyone, "fight, fight for the future, for the children, for your parents, your family, the person holding your hand," people cheered; it felt like everything was possible: "the streets are ours," &

I became a Whitman song, '"Oh me! Oh life! that I am here," a time of angels, a weightlessness took me, & here we all are, except the people who are still in camps, who are slowly being forgotten in posters on city walls, in newspapers, Facebook, Instagram, Twitter, & the families' photos back at home.

I still have that feeling in the city center square, but it's broken from living history, from reading about all the people who disappeared in the 20th century from wars, from governments, from cops, & who are still disappearing—after all of it, I feel like *Coyolxauhqui,* goddess of the Milky Way, who was butchered by her brother, *Huitzilopochtli,* the god of war. She lived on in perseverance but in pieces. *Amá,* I guess to know the whole, we must be broken, let the healing transform us, like Kintsugi, the art of repairing broken pottery with gold: it shines the way stars do, how it's fractured but still gleams, & holds everything, like you still do, all these years.

III

Border Walls

that	be	mem
get	name	hear,
te:	na	Grief:
a	from	&
bor	dy.	&
lang	cher	ed,
ders	be	ors
ders	amp	is
man	one	moon.

How many pe	died when building	wall & how ma
people were kill	from the wall? Mil	ons of human
nes have been fou	underneath the	at wall. In th
eof law, over	ion acres of	& their commun
ties of life are	pled by man,	where a visitor,
not remain, but	borders do. Onc	year, I lived on
Tio's farm In	*nillo, Zaca*	as; he would mend
neighbor's fences	a border of	es & cactus.
prima says she	never visit	the border, nev

wish   pen   *juan*

er   den,   the

bees,   birds   ders.

ev   tle   be

qui   are   ra

juan   used   pe

to   talk,   both

&   ers,   Pa

a   be   it

is impossi to meet the peo on the other

Over seven and people have d crossing th

S borders; bo never get re ered, over sev

thousand left be borders. To live this side of th

der that believes "good fences make neighbors," to

foot walls made of lectrified fen along miles

miles of o deserts, in bet are hundreds

osks, thousands of veillance cameras a relentless

ga	*ha*	*bien*
fron	*me*	*ol*
ma	*mos*	*ia:*
char,	*sa*	*ex*
nac	*ras.*	*Pe*
de	*de*	*s*
es	*fron*	*po.*
y	*s*	*i*
ser	*y*	*ya*
as	*e*	*a*
do	*ba*	*des*
ej	*Mu*	*ún*
hu	*tie*	*de*

ver desde la   na. ¿Cuántas per   as murieron al

struir el mu   y cuántas per   as fueron as

inadas? Se   encontrado   ones de hues

humanos de   jo de la gran   ralla. En nom

de la ley, más   un millón de   res de tierra

sus comuni   des de vida   pisoteadas

el hombre,   de el hombre,   visitante

permanece,   ro las fronte   sí. Una vez

año, después   que papá se   vivía en

granja de mi   o en Fresni   Zacatecas;

repararí   las cercas de   vecino con

borde de ro   y cactus. Mi   ma dice

ca visita   a frontera,   nunca más de

bra	*a*	*en*
de	*ni*	*do,*
y	*el*	*dí*
ma	*a*	*la*
s.	*zan*	*dos*
sua	*de*	*es*
que	*e*	*e.*
a	*so*	*a*
er	*fron*	*bla*
se	*su*	*des*
la	*mer,*	*bra*
de	*Pa*	*ri*
a	*bi*	*io*

ntermedio, r lo que a ra es impos

ble conocer la gente del ro lado. Más

siete mil per nas murieron zando las fron

ras de Esta s Unidos ntre 1998

2016; gunos cuerpos ca se recu

an, quedan más iete mil en ronteras. Pa

vivir en es lado de la era que cree

"buenas cercas cen buenos ve os", tener pa

des de diez pies has de cercas lectrifica

s, a lo lar de millas y as de desier

abiertos, en dio hay cientos quioscos,

les de cáma de vigilan a observan

un bri im c

IV

Watching a Video of Earth from the ISS Live Feed

La tierra can look so foreign

craters

homes I'll never live in

& I know life is a long sentence

made of links, sounds, clauses,

how the clouds constantly move

into yesterday, from today, into tomorrow,

again, & again, & again,

look how small everything is,

hold it

like the page holds these words,

how you hold

these words

in you

Ameriposx, a **Flower Song**

a plumed femme in a teal sun dress,
pintada in *yoliliztli* & dazzle shadow,

with a body like a *pambazo, de papas y chorizo,*
& in the *Loteria*, I would be *la rosa, la calavera, el mundo,*

el apache, la sirena, la muerte & the whole damn deck,
& when I'm buried below, I'll be so many names:

helianthus, Paeonia lactiflora, Xolotl;
ants will live in the moans of me, a colony

built by mandibles, their worlds built in mouths
& before this world goes eternal, I'll continue to sing

in a, e. i, o, u,
our words building blocks,

they let me live
inside our skies,

& I start to know the gift of poets:
hungry, all gods live off of us

Fuji Apples

For Lupe

I finally kiss them,
didn't know I could,

Jesús Cristo never kissed
disciples on the lips,

nor did men or women kiss
in my history books

& then we smoke weed
through an apple,

we received each other's shape
& moan the way trees creak

from the roots, my tongue
traces an outline of their body,

a sound like a snail on a leaf,
rounds out of my mouth

Dear Cuñada,

Pues, children are in cages, expected to defend themselves in court *Cuñada*, kids that look like your son, who asked me, "where do we come from?" *Cuñada*,

I told him some say we fell from the sky, some say we were made from clay, others say corn, while others say we are living in a dream. *Cuñada*

I don't want this dream where brothers, sisters, cousins are in cages & say, *this is where I come from*. To believe this is all legal *Cuñada*,

forced in camps, I mean jails, I mean cages, I mean processing centers, crammed together on floor mats in plastic-shrouded rooms *Cuñada*.

officials admitted, "these are not places made for children," but for aliens,
not ones that fell from the sky, or made of clay or corn, but niños *Cuñada,*

that know 2 + 2 = 4, that can say the word, flower, & can say the A, B C's,
who sing, row, row, row, your boat, life is but a dream, if only, right *Cuñada?*

Staring at the Sky

Para mi Tía Esperanza

I can't stop looking at the clouds. It reminds me of your name: *Esperanza*, a movement *Tía*,
like wind passing through trees, flowers, & grass; we are all these moments *Tía*,

I trust water more than I do people. When drunk, it sings a garden inside of me.
I feel it swishing in my mouth; this instant is worth a thousand tomorrows *Tía*,

the way your body echoes: a voyage of planets, meteorites, stars—things that survive
to paint the world around us, worlds that we'll never have futures in *Tía*,

we all see the same when our eyes close, but when open: the world calls
season after season, they say, lay in me, warm and grow, grow—*Tía*,

all atoms & particles in the universe behave like waves, including all the atoms
that we ourselves are made of, waves are at the very nature of our reality *Tía*,

beyond this, do we still dance? Remember you & little me, dancing to *Cómo te voy a olvidar,* the way you moved: at sunrise, shadows riding leaves in the wind. It's always real for me *Tía.*

Primo Pancho's Corrido

I'm from wild ones on the corner of Pierce & De Foe
with atom-smashing tattoos on arms for each year in juvie

earshot of *bachata palabras* about their next fix,
who at night walk by graveyard guards

finding brown bottles filled with silence in their beds,
who drive past glass smoking junkies who die with stars

silently singing, *una copa mas*, their voices
like names autographed on concrete;

I'm from the projects sundry colored LEGOs,
blazon joints in zip bags, mouth-drum moms,

those with bullet-tongues & baleen teeth,
who ask for change under the 118 freeway,

from *vagabondos* on nowhere shorelines,
& the *nopaleros* who had nothing

but dirt-hearts & 99¢ dreams

The 92 Bus

I wake up at three a.m., shower, brush my teeth,
but forget to pack my lunch & put on make-up,

but I continue to live,
to learn every day

everything is always new to me,
like sunlight that has been traveling years

to my face on the next stop. Someone's
always at work: people who monitor the buses,

garbage workers who pick up our trash,
sanitation crew dispose our waste,

security guards who walk through museums,
& the rest of us, here, going somewhere,

& I know how it feels to make a dollar outta' 15 cents
as 2pac said, but I'm exhausted by being

by working 50-hour work weeks, feeding
myself at Food Not Bombs at *Gonzales* Park,

making sure to be in the vale of soul-making,
It takes its toll when I can't afford my Lexapro,

& who told the universe to quantum?
I look up: we're all moving, being led

by what came before us, & on my day off
in a few more days: smells of weed,

four *lokos*, fried *nopales,* the sage smoke
burns the week away, the good & bad,

everything eventually dies so they can become again,
but before I clock in, I buy a cup of coffee, burn myself

& wait for sun rays, so my skin can eat,
& maybe see a rainbow today

Tagging on the Side of a Wendy's

Where are all the Native American statues?

If you were an algorithm   how long would you be?

Cash rules everything around me

No soy de aquí

ni soy de allá

Horizons are always giving

So many sighs

Yo tambien estoy jodido

Plan or be planned for

"I imagine light in a way that you can't."

Who you give your money to is who you give your power to

I guess god didn't want me to be rich

How many times can a wall be repainted?

Are we someone's background music?

AN AIRPLANE PULLS A GIANT AD THROUGH THE SKY SAYING: PEPSI, DRINK IT.

Our cellphones are always listening,
I keep getting ads from the marines & Pizza Hut,

don't they know I'm lactose & non-violent?
Another ad says, what's your plan to be rich?

One week I didn't understand English & good morning
looked like someone trying to suck my whole body,

then talking looked like piano keys playing
free form jazz: controlled, raw, how a wolf eats a kill.

Eventually I understood when an officer said, "Open the bag. Now."
But life is good *amá*. I dated a person who liked to dance,

I told them The Smiths should be made into *cumbia*,
imagine: Sheila take a Sheila take a bow, taka ta taka ta taka ta,

pues, being lactose intolerant sucks, I can't have ice cream or brie,
but at least the planets all sing in their own keys I can hear, look:

Saturn   Jupiter   Mars, nearly   The Earth

Venus   Mercury   Here the Moon also
has a place.

I never thought we would listen to the heavens & still be sane,
but we do come from them, so it only makes sense we understand.

I found out there are black holes the size of forty Earth suns, they eat everything,
even light. Remember when the panama papers came out & revealed

all the rich people in the world are part of an enormous criminal conspiracy
to dodge taxes, hoard stolen wealth in offshore accounts & nothing happened,

I'm having trouble inventing my future when nobody wants it

Dear *Primo José*,

Last night I dreamt you directed a movie: luminous plastic
rolls around alleyways, snail shells held by your hand,

then you were drumming: high hat, base bat, snare snap,
while your feet soft heel-down, heavy down-heeled,

& then you were drinking two-gallon screwdrivers
in a '95 Astro van, with *Sepultura* cranked up,

you were head banging till you were all whiplash,
but I woke up, recalled when I got the call,

they told me you were found,
                            found

moments are enormous,
a sweetness

to hold on to,
I'm surprised

we ever found words
for silence,

how deep it nerves,
constant it gathers,

present,
a willing,

it is ever
that surrounds,

every year
I moment you,

the fullness:
a distance,

how it grows

I'm Not Sorry for Being Human & Smoking a Joint While Watching Planet Earth

When my nephew was born, he was soft, tiny, & quiet— I was afraid to hold him,

but then I did, & I cried.

He comes from Immigrants, the word comes from the Latin, *migrare*:

to move from one place to another to another,

sentences are all immigrants,

look at them moving to the page to eyes to brains to throats,

& *amás* citizenship papers saying she's legal here, though earth never refused.

I look at my nephew's drawing of our family on my phone: outlines in brown

& black crayons on construction paper, you know that leaves built altars for the sun

from their bodies, luminance eaten daily, & when trees are chopped down to make paper,

their bodies sing out in O's—

we have been writing on the sun all this time, how it speaks: a lesson in instance:

nourishments, joys, reactions, violences, occurrences of the present,

outside, I can't un-see everything, it keeps saying: I'm alive

Para Mis Chiquistriquis
For B and N

So much your eyes don't see: oxygen
breathed in by dinosaurs & Australopithecus,

flowers that have eaten more sun than we ever will.
Pick up a *papaya*, cut it in half, let seeds spill, juices run,

bite into the sunset of its body, taste the horizon,
& once a year, outline your hands on a piece of paper.

In ten years you'll see how hands can grow like trees,
& don't forget to sing the songs of your *abuelitos*,

like this one*, amor eterno, e inolvidable, tarde
o temprano estare contigo, para seguir, amándos.*

On this day your bodies are a testimonial like spiral sea shells,
your names, an inheritance, like the palms your parents gifted you,

but promise me, *mis chiquistriquis, mi queridxs, mis estrellas,*
when I'm no longer here, read me a poem on my birthday,

so my bones can feel again

Dear *Hermanita*,

Your *pan dulce* body: a soft marvel

no one can replicate like fireflies

in summer nights: they beam

their glow to a planet

filled with gold grass, mercury oceans,

a gelatinous family looking above them,

the way our *familia* held you above us

when you were a baby— *Hermanita*,

who loves you more than your family?

An always waiting for you in your *corazón*,

asking you, what new fact you learned in the world,

like light never stops but it can be absorbed

when it hits us, it continues to glow,

like your *familia's* love for you

Dear *Hermano,*

Again people are being taken away,
I read the news of kids
like your daughter & son,
like our family, our neighbors,

they wake in a state of temporary,
that lasts longer & longer &
longer than we can remember.
I read online the Smithsonian

purchased children's drawings
of them in camps: grey beds,
red, black, & orange people in them,
archaeology happening in real time.

Is remembrance joy? I once asked *abuela,*
she said, "It takes work until it becomes
second nature to you, like breathing,
like knowing the earth gave you a voice

to sing across generations like this:
in t'aane, lu'um, in t'aane, lu'um
kun k'ayik in k'ajláayn in t'aane
lu'um, in t'aane, lu'um.

the clouds look
like they're going on forever;
do they ever die?
or are they constantly reincarnating?

Life, *aqui*, a deep possibility,
of memories: a translation of living,
a brief swell of air along a saguaro's needles,
the way we eat: alive,

but *hermano*, there are still camps,
& when I'm eating a fruit salad, I crunch
into the body of lettuce, the crispness
has a cost, but all of this always did, remember?

Dear *Amá,*

"You can't jail a revolution" was tagged on the side of a Wendy's,
but *amá*, you can make it go into debt & never revolt,

who can afford to move into the future
when today is always catching up?

I bite into a taste of home: deep fried dough *con azúcar,*
churros sold by a couple that look like your parents,

you told me *abuelo* mined the underworld for ancient memories
worth millions of dollars under our feet, all his years digging

cost less than all the minerals he dug out.
You asked him, "Why do we wear the stars?"

You said he laughed, coughed up his lungs,
but looking at the night sky, I want to wear it,

that everywhere where dreams are made real,
where the oldest things to survive are like a heart,

with four chambers, the flow sings a remembrance.
to keep us from exiting ourselves, like a promise

to stop eating fried food for a whole year, but *sopes*,
asada fries, pueeeesss, maybe I'll try again next year,

& why do two hydrogen love one oxygen: to let us inhale
one of the oldest contracts of the universe: air,

it carries the smells of everything, like jasmine,
lavender, pine trees, a new book when it opens

for the first time: there's matter & energy in there,
like our final hug when we last saw each other,

I still feel it now, the way we held each other: a uni –
verse, a womb that creates, births & emerges

traces of tomorrows, the stars

V

Greyhound Americans

Tía Carmen came 363 miles
North   only to be
pulled over   cuffed
sent to the box

Primo Oscar yells
Belief equals everything
we knows it
president knows it
vatos knows it
you knows it too

Tía Martha bleeds yellow
in fields of iceberg lettuce
it haunts the basement of my skin

Mi abuelo once said   gods say we must appease company
but it seems certain guests
take more than we can afford to give

Walking through *Tijuana*
faces bloom
in through chain link fences

Tio Kiko says each leaf
is trying their best
to green

Tío Urbano said
your *Tía's* hair
I'll never see again

Mi abuelita said   the last star of the night   ends in morning

I shovel the soil with both hands
hold it to the sky
streams from my fingers
I hear my name

the way it falls
an oath
to return
to remember

Infinite Gratitude

To my *abuelos*: *Maria "Conchita" Aguilar, Juanita Zamora Alvarado, & Fidencio Davila Escobedo*. Without you, there wouldn't be, *mi familia*.

To my *Amá*, for all her love, sacrifice, endurance; for teaching me how to hustle when I was young with that swap meet life; to singing *Paquita La Del Barrio & Juan Gabriel* while cleaning apartments & houses. Thank you again to all the trips to the library after you came out of work. *Mi hermano*, for your kindness; leading with love when it comes to living your life with your family. And *mi hermanita and Scott*, for your courage to pursue your dreams, *chisme* on the phone, your internet memes, & abundance of love to our family. To my sister-in-law Janet and Scott thank you for showing me kindness, love, & care. To Benny & Natalia, for the unconditional love you show me every time I see, hear, & laugh with you.

Para Mi Escobedo 's; primero mis tias: Carmen, Alicia, Elisa, Esther, Chela, Pera. Mis tios: Kiko, Arturo, Wilfredo, Urbano, Alvaro, Juan. Primo & Primas: Diego, Liz, Carlos, Cisco, Art, Diana, Mayo, Marcos, Guecho, Crystal, Cynthia, Chuy, Pera, Lili, Itzel, Nessie, Maria Carmen, Willie Jr, & Mandis. Thank you to you all always for the lessons in endure in the toughest of times, through your love & support.

Pari mi Gonzalez's: Tia Martha, Lalo, Cecilia, Rocio, Dario, Pancho, Joaquin, Tetos, Laura, Patty, & all their kids. Thank you to you all for the lessons to endure with love, support, & laughs that turned into ugly crying, then ugly laughing.

Mi Alvarado's: Jesus, Cleme, Juanita, Juan Jose, Pilar, Paulina, Luis, Belina, Juan, Antonio, Edgar, Karina, Pipis, Vickie, Teresa, Lule, Esperanza, Pepe, Ra-

mon, & Pachita. Thank you for your help along the way when this was just lyrics in metal songs when I stayed in *Zamora as a teenager.*

To Diane Seuss & the folx at Saturnalia Books for choosing me, you made this girl's dream come true. This is real & in my hands, I can not thank you enough for this gift, this chance, these flower songs to be out in the world. Thank you to Sarah & Robin for your kindness & care with my words.

Thanks to Troika House: *Adrian, Maria, Socorro, Salvador, Trinidad,* & *Gloria.* Thank you for having me, for taking care of me, & supporting my art.

To The Band & all the fellas: *Diego, Oscar, Julio, Ricardo, Jesus,* for your enduring care, support, yearly last waltzes, & for always singin' with me, "oh, to be home again, down in Pacoima." Thanks as well to *Monse, JOSHUA JESSIE GONZALES* & *Freddy Garcia,* who were always there for me when I needed to talk & stay grounded.

My Mentors who showed me I was light & flowers: Tina Chang, Cathy Park Hong, Aracelis Girmay, Randall Horton, Ryka Aoki, Martin Pousson, Dorothy Barresi, & Kate Haake.

Helen Wurlitzer Foundation *familia*: Nic Knight, Mitch, Marcos, Maria, Shawn, Rebecca, Cyrus. Thank you Nic for letting me finish this collection. Thank you Cyrus, for the sage advice you gave me on my first day. Thank you Shawn, for showing me the beauty of The Rift in Taos.

Poets House familia: Haydil, Sébastien, Joel, Cindy, Sarah, Thiahera, Trace, Sokunthary, & my dear sister in residence in movement, Jasmine. To the folx at Poets house that helped me: thank you, and to the library: Oh, the time I spent reading, communing.

Thank you my Lambda familia: Wryly, Catherine, Aurielle, Cori, Dana, Hank, Jaz, Jon, Nefertiti, KB, Victoria, Mariam, Melissa, Natasha, Kay. Thank you William & Sue, for giving me a chance at being a fellow & being part of this family.

My TJ's crews at 533, 122, & 547; from morning, to mid, to closing, to overnight shifts, seeing you all live & work was inspirational.

My animal kids, *Chucho* & Pigeon, for waking me up early to read, write, edit, walk you, & feed you. To my wonderful partner, wife, leader of team Tomo, & The Snack Pack Crew, Toni. I am grateful you choose me & continue to do so every day.

To my community, my friends: *Alice, Rob, Lizzy, Lupe, Chunks, Pia, Loredo, Ceci, Elizabeth, Geo, Donna, Jorge, Ez, Bernie, Solia, Connie, the Vadillos, Noel, Naomi, Jasmine, Luz, Zero, Tony, Slip, Luis, Paige, Amparo, Jeff, Jordan, Derek, Sreshtha, Tara, Cody, Kevin, Kris, Alexandra, Jimena, Cristian, Gina, Sean, Vickie, Latasha, Ben, Robin, Zefyr, Heidi, Susanna, Ricardo, Momo, Shayla, Steve, Maeve, Dimirti, Monica, Alexis, Danilo, Anatalia, Morgan, Omotara, Cornelius, Yanyi, Paulo, Gia, Cynthia, Shane, Marwa, Ricardo, Aldrin, Purvi, Jose, Leon, Xochitl, Vanessa, Danny, Rigoberto, Gabriela, Rita, Joseph, Jill,* The Nuggies, The LP, & everyone else that helped me along the way.

To the *Tataviam, Tongva, Gila River, Taos Pueblo, Choctaw, Lenape, P'urhépecha, Maya Yucateco, Mēxihcah* & *Zacateco* peoples, on whose occupied territory I have lived, been nurtured by, & helped me finish this dream in my hands.

Acknowledgements

Endless thank you to editors and readers of the following publications for publishing many of the poems in this collection, often in different versions.

Acentos Review: "Beneath Me"

Already Felt: "*Ameriposx*, A Flower Song"

Bellevue Literary Review: "Three Eagles Flying"

Borderlands: Texas Poetry Review: "Dear *Amá* (I keep getting ads…)"

Breadcrumbs: "Happy Father's Day *Amá* "

Chaparral: "Sounds"

Dryland Literary Journal: "Helping my Mom Practice for Her Citizenship Test" "Pigeons" "*Amá* Teaches Me How to Whistle"

Foglifter: "How I Eat the Stars"

Hayden's Ferry Review: "Dear Bernie" and "Dear *Amá* (This Body is an instrument…)"

LAMBDA Fellows Anthology 2018: "*Mi Gente*" and "Questions for an ESL…" and "Check boxes that apply…"

Lunch Ticket: "Building the Backyard House with *Abuelo*"

Meridian: "Dear *Amá* (You can't jail a revolution...)"

Michigan Quarterly Review: "Payday Inside the Projects"

Mikrokosmosjournal: "Fuji Apples"

Northridge Review: "Cube" and "*Pacoima Corrido*"

Poetry Project House Party #5: "I'm Not Sorry for Smoking a Joint While Watching Planet
Earth" and "*Mi Gente*, A Portrait"

Poets House: "*Taco* Tuesday"

Poets.org: "Sift"

Puerto del Sol: "My *Amá* After Work, a Portrait" and "Dear *Amá* (When I confessed top you...)"

Rumpus: "At Eight" and "September 1996"

Tahoma Literary Review : "*Para Mis Chiquistriquis*"

About the Author

Moncho Alvarado is a sister-in-residence-in-air, a Cihuayollotl trans woman Xicanx poet, translator, visual artist, and educator. She is the author of *Greyhound Americans* (Saturnalia Books 2022), which was the winner of the 2020 Saturnalia Book Prize, selected by Diane Seuss. She has been published in Meridian, Foglifter, Lunch Ticket, 2018 Emerge Lambda Fellows Anthology, Poets.org, and other publications. She is a recipient of fellowships and residencies from The Helene Wurlitzer Foundation, Lambda Literary, Poets House, Troika House, the Summer Seminar at Sarah Lawrence College, and won the Academy of American Poet's John B. Santoianni award for excellence in poetry. She is pushcart nominated and has been awarded the Thomas Lux Scholarship for dedication to teaching, demonstrated through writing workshops with youths in Sunnyside Community Services in Queens, New York. Find her at monchoalvarado.com

Greyhound Americans is printed in Baskerville and Adobe Garamond Pro.
www.saturnaliabooks.org